Stewarding God's Story in Your Life

It's Your Story But It's About Jesus

La'Treall Maddox

Ox & Maven

Copyright

Published by Ox & Maven | New York, NY, USA

www.oxandmaven.com

Cover and interior design by Ox & Maven | Printed in The United States of America

ISBN: 979-8-9996730-0-8 (Paperback) 979-8-9996730-1-5 (Digital)

Dedication

To Jesus—Who rescued me, rewrote my story, and taught me to share it

To Granny and to Colton—whose lives bookend the beginning and becoming of this work

Contents

Foreword

by Pastor Justin Lewandowski, Brooklyn Tabernacle

We live in a time when personal stories are shared constantly - accomplishments, travels, daily routines - all broadcast to the world in real time. While these stories may offer brief moments of connection or inspiration, most will fade from memory over time. But there is one story that will last for all eternity, and that's your personal story of God's redemptive power. The idea for this book - originally conceived as a workshop - was born from a deeper burden: to help people tell the most important story of their lives - the story of their redemption.

After years of watching people try to share or write their testimonies, I realized how many struggled to articulate the significance of what God had done in their lives. That realization sparked the vision for a class or workshop. I had the idea, but I didn't yet know how to bring it to life. Through prayer and divine providence, God led me to La'Treall. We had already spent time discussing various discipleship tools. When I presented the concept to her, she immediately embraced it.

At first, she thought it would be simple - just a matter of adapting content from existing books. What we quickly discovered was that there were few resources that truly captured the heart of what we wanted to accomplish. So instead of borrowing someone else's framework, La'Treall began building one from the ground up.

Over the course of several months, she took a single thought and developed a rich, multi-part workshop. Its purpose was to help people not only understand how God brought them to salvation but also recognize how He continues writing new chapters in their lives as they grow into maturity in Christ.

The process was not without challenges. Every step seemed to be met with resistance - spiritual, emotional, logistical. That's the nature of the enemy of our souls. He does not want believers to share the second most powerful story after the Gospel itself: the personal testimony of transformation - God bringing someone from spiritual death to life, from bondage to freedom. Yet we prayed, pushed forward, and watched God bring this work to completion.

We began with a small pilot group made up of ministries we believed would benefit most. The response was powerful. Many participants shared that, for the first time, they felt truly equipped to share their story of salvation with clarity and confidence.

Encouraged by the results, we opened the training to the broader church. Hundreds came. The hunger was evident - people were eager to learn how to express what God had done, and was still doing, in their lives. Some attendees even urged us to take the workshop to other churches and cities. While we were humbled by that suggestion, neither of us felt called to start a traveling ministry.

Instead, God gave birth to another idea - this time through La'Treall: transform the workshop into a book. A resource that could be shared broadly, used by churches, small groups, and individuals alike.

And that's what you now hold in your hands.

This book is designed to help you reflect on your journey, recognize the hand of God at work, and share your testimony with clarity and purpose. Whether you're reading it for personal growth or to lead others, we pray it encourages you to record what God has done - is doing - in your life. But more than recording it, may you boldly share your story with a world longing for hope. Because through your story, others may come to know the Author of redemption for themselves. That Author is Jesus.

Introduction

I want to begin by saying this plainly: if you've struggled to share your testimony, you are not alone.

> "God is not looking for brilliant people, He is looking for broken people who are willing to be used."
>
> — Jim Cymbala, 1997, p. 133

Even now, seasoned believers who've shared their testimony many times often feel a jolt of uncertainty when someone says, "Tell us your story." A wave of questions floods in: *Which part? Where do I begin? How much time do I have?* And underneath those questions is something deeper - a reverence. A holy weight. Because we know we are not just recounting memories or building rapport. We are speaking about the moment when the LORD stepped into our lives and saved us. And we don't want to treat that lightly.

Part of that holy weight comes from remembering that we don't all hear stories the same way. As Jason Georges explains in *The 3D Gospel*, different cultures often see the world through different primary lenses: guilt and innocence, shame and honor, or fear and power. In one setting, your testimony might land most deeply when you talk about God's forgiveness and cleansing. In another, it might resonate most when you share how He restored your honor and belonging. In yet another, it could be when you speak of His power to free and protect you. We'll revisit these ideas later, but even now, keep in mind — the way you tell your story can help it connect to the listener's deepest need.

I've spent the last several years listening to others wrestle with how to share their testimony. I've struggled with this myself. I've lived the discomfort of being unsure what to say or how to say it. I've heard people say things like:

- "I don't remember when I got saved, so do I even have a testimony?"
- "My story's boring - God didn't rescue me from drugs or prison."
- "I'm still struggling with stuff. I don't want to be a hypocrite."
- "I don't want to air my family's business."
- "I'm not good with words."
- "It's too painful to talk about."

Sometimes, the reason is shame. Other times, it's uncertainty. But almost always, there's a sense of *disqualification*. As if only certain kinds of stories *count*.

That's a lie from the enemy.

One of the most common tactics Satan uses is to silence the people of God. He whispers, *You have nothing to say. You're still too messy. Your story isn't enough. No one will believe you.* But Scripture tells a different story:

> "And they overcame and conquered him because of the blood of the Lamb and because of the word of their testimony..." Revelation 12:11a (AMP)

This verse is more than poetic. It's powerful. The blood of Jesus and the word of our testimony - working together - are how the saints overcome the enemy.

Your testimony is not a performance. It's not about impressing others or even proving a point.

It's a witness.

And God, in His sovereignty, has entrusted it to you.

When the idea for this testimony training first began to stir in my heart, I thought it would be simple. Just gather a few scriptures, some prompts, and examples from others. But what God led me to do was much deeper. This wasn't just about teaching people how to write a personal narrative. It was about reorienting our understanding of what it means to *steward* the stories He's written in our lives.

In the Church, we often talk about stewarding our time, talent, and treasure. But our testimony is a fourth "T" that often gets overlooked. And I believe the LORD is calling His people to steward it well - not to hide it out of fear or shame, but to share it with discernment, boldness, and compassion.

Introduction

In this book, we'll walk through why your story matters, how to shape it, when and where to share it, and how to listen for the Holy Spirit's prompting. You'll also have space to reflect, journal, and practice - not to perfect your story, but to become more attentive to what God has done and how He might use it for someone else's freedom.

Because here's the truth:

Faith is personal - but it's never private.

Your testimony is not yours to keep. It's a gift to share. And you don't need to wait until it feels easier or your life looks better. The same God Who saved you is still writing your story. And He's already prepared someone who will believe in Him - because *of the message He gave to you.*

Let's begin.

Chapter 1

Shoshana – Something Missing

Some people meet Jesus in a moment. Others recognize His hand only in hindsight — after years of going through the motions, years of spiritual striving, years not realizing something was missing. For Shoshana, that recognition came gradually. It wasn't the absence of faith that shaped her story — it was the slow undoing of a system that looked like faith but left no room for relationship. This is a story about God's patience, His pursuit, and the power of surrender when you've run out of your own strength.

Shoshana's Testimony

I grew up in a family that loved God. My dad was a praying man — I'd see him on his knees. My mom loved the LORD too, but raising kids made regular church attendance a little harder. Still, God was around us.

My oldest sister went to Catholic school and because she had to attend Catholic church, I started going with her. I was the baby — the one who tagged along for everything. And I stayed for years. I became active in the Catholic church. I followed all the rules — no meat on Fridays, regular confession, teaching in Catholic schools. I was all in. But when the Pope started changing things — saying now it's okay to eat meat on Fridays, that confession wasn't required the same way — I got confused. I thought, Did God change?

That's when the LORD started opening my eyes. I realized: I didn't actually know

Him. I'd never read the Bible. I followed rituals, but I didn't have a relationship. It had felt safe — comfortable even — but something was missing.

A friend kept inviting me to her church and eventually I went. The worship was different. It wasn't just hymns — it was praise. There was joy! I kept going. I got more involved. And one day, my daughter said something I'll never forget. The pastor had said something that felt racially divisive. My daughter looked at me and asked, "Doesn't God love *everybody*?" That was it. That's when I knew I couldn't stay.

I started going to another church — and for the first time, I felt the presence of God, not just the form of religion. I'd walk into prayer meetings and feel the weight of the Holy Spirit. The atmosphere was different. It was alive. It made me want more. My old church didn't understand — they said, "*This* is your church, why are you leaving?" But I knew the LORD was doing something new in me.

That season changed me. I started seeing people differently. One day, I passed a man on the street and I sensed the LORD tell me, "Tell him I love him." I kept walking. But by the time I reached my car, the prompting was so strong I turned around and returned to where the man was. I told him. He smiled. I didn't have fancy words. Just obedience. That moment opened something in me.

Eventually, I began serving in shelters — feeding women, hugging them, praying for them. And the LORD had to deal with me. I had issues — I was too prissy, too cautious. But He healed me. Taught me to touch what I once avoided. To see people through His eyes. To show up. Even after long workdays, even when it felt like nothing was changing.

One night I sat at a prayer meeting and whispered to God, "Is there any fruit in what I'm doing?" A young woman was sitting beside me and said, "I know you. You brought me from the shelter to visit church one day. I'm still coming — and I gave my life to Jesus." The words had barely left my lips and the Holy Spirit had answered.

And then — my health shifted. I lost the sight in my right eye. They never figured out why. A decade later, I lost use of my right hand. That's when they diagnosed me with multiple sclerosis — in my late 60s. It was a shock because it usually shows up much sooner. But I call it a different way of living, not an illness. The LORD has been so kind. I was in the hospital during the pandemic, but I had my own room with a beautiful view. It felt like a vacation. I was so well cared for. That was my Father — setting a table for me even there in the hospital.

When I left the hospital, they sent me home because of visitor restrictions during the pandemic. I remember thinking, "I'm going home in what feels like a limo!" The LORD just kept blessing me — through the nurses, the room, the timing. He even gave me a neurologist who doesn't know Him yet — but he's watching. He keeps asking how I'm still going. I tell him: "I know Who's holding me." I get to share Jesus.

I still have struggles. I'm a fixer. I want to help everyone. But the LORD keeps reminding me: It's not you. It's Me. It's really a pronoun issue. Not "I," but "He." That's how I want to live now.

Reflection: Doorway To Something Deeper

Shoshana's story is a reminder that form without God's presence is a poor substitute for faith. She had rituals. She had reverence. But she didn't have Jesus — not yet. It wasn't until the rules changed, and her questions deepened, that she started looking for something more.

And the LORD met her — not in shame, but in revelation. He didn't reject her former devotion. He used it as a doorway to something deeper. That's who He is.

"Draw near to God, and He will draw near to you" (James 4:8a). He's not distant. He's not hiding. He reveals Himself to those who are willing to surrender what they thought they knew.

And that surrender has marked every part of her journey — from feeding the homeless to hugging women in shelters, from laying down control to living with what others label as chronic illness. But she doesn't see it as loss. She calls it blessing. Even the hospital stay. Even the unanswered questions. Even the unmet longings.

Why? Because she knows Who is writing her story — and He's not finished yet.

And maybe, like Shoshana, you've been doing all the right things but wondering why it still feels empty. Maybe your faith has been more about doing than knowing. The invitation is open: Trade striving for surrender. Let the form and function give way to the presence of knowing God as your Father. And listen for the voice Who says: "Tell them I love them."

Chapter 2

Why Your Story Matters

"Let the redeemed of the
LORD tell their story -
those He has redeemed
from the hand of the
foe."

— Psalm 107:2 NIV

Your testimony is the personal story God has authored in your life. It is a gift - entrusted to you - for the purpose of sharing. And like any gift He gives, it's meant to be stewarded with intention and care. That doesn't mean broadcasting it constantly or forcing your experiences into every conversation. It means being available and willing, led by the Holy Spirit, to speak truthfully about how Jesus has saved and shaped your life. That willingness is part of our kingdom assignment.

Every believer receives a special gift from Jesus - the personal story He has authored in our lives. That story, our testimony, is entrusted to us to share with others.

A testimony is more than a personal story. It's a declaration - a witness - of what Jesus has done. It's not about achievements or self-improvement. It's not a spiritual résumé. It's a personal account of God's redemptive power at work. In fact, the word "testimony" itself comes from legal language. It means to give evidence, to bear witness to the truth. In both Scripture and modern law, a testimony carries weight. It can change the outcome of a trial. It can determine what is believed.

The same is true in the spiritual realm.

According to Merriam-Webster, a testimony is:

- A solemn declaration usually made orally by a witness under oath
- Firsthand authentication of a fact
- An open acknowledgment
- A public profession of a religious experience

And for believers, it's all of these. But it's also something more.

- It's a personal account of what God has done in your life.
- It's more about the work of Jesus and less about personal accomplishments.
- It's your opportunity to point to

the Gospel - not just in theory, but in your lived reality.

We do not share our testimony to be admired. We share it to glorify God the Father, to exalt Jesus, and in obedience to the Holy Spirit's leading. Our lives bear witness to His grace, His mercy, and His power to redeem.

The moment we think our testimony is about us, we've missed the point of sharing it. The purpose is not to recount every mistake or highlight every success. It's to point to the One who saves.

It's to say, "This is what Jesus did in me. This is who I was. This is who I'm becoming - because of Him."

God is writing a story in your life that is meant to be told - not hidden. It's His story, written in your chapters.

And that's why your story matters.

Not because it's dramatic. Not because it's tidy. But because it reveals the goodness of God - and invites others to know Him, too.

Questions for Reflection

1. What comes to mind when you hear the word "testimony"? Has that changed over time?
2. What makes you hesitate to share your story?
3. What do you think God wants others to know about Him through what He's done in your life?
4. Who shared their testimony with you - and how did it impact your faith?
5. How might your testimony serve someone else's breakthrough?

Prayer Point

LORD, thank You for the story You are writing in my life. Thank You for redeeming me - not just to be saved, but to be a witness. Help me steward the testimony You've given me with clarity, humility, and courage. May every word I share point to Your glory. Amen.

Chapter 3

Braha – A Light from the Night

She grew up in a Muslim country. Her family wasn't devout, but religion was in the air — and so was fear. What began as a child's curiosity with a children's animated Bible series slowly unfolded into a decades-long spiritual chase, marked by trauma, questions, and invisible protection she didn't yet recognize. She carried fear like a shadow — fear of death, fear of rejection, fear of not being enough.

But the God of the Bible — the One she had once only seen through the lens of animations and colored pages — would not let her go.

It wasn't a flash of light or a single moment that changed her. It was the slow, steady pursuit of Jesus — a pursuit that reshaped how she saw sin, family, forgiveness, and the very nature of love.

Braha's Testimony

I grew up in a Muslim country. My family wasn't religious — we were culturally Muslim, but no one actually practiced. We would go to the mosque during holidays, but I never liked it. I never wanted to be Muslim. I was rebellious against all of it.

My father was addicted to drugs and alcohol. It made everything hard. He was aggressive and I hated what he did to my mother. I used to wish he would die. That's how angry I was. I was five when I started to understand how broken things were in my family.

On top of that, there was darkness in my home. My father's mother who lived with us — my grandmother — practiced witchcraft. She did rituals, cursed us, threw animal remains at our door. She hated my mother. She wanted my parents to separate.

I left home as soon as I could. After university, I moved to another city — not because I loved someone, but because I needed a way out. I told my family I was in a relationship and that became my excuse. The man was culturally Muslim, but I didn't care. It wasn't about him. I just couldn't stay in that environment any longer back home.

I've carried fear my whole life. Fear of dying. Fear of flying. Fear of sleeping. Fear of hell. Even as a child, I was terrified. I knew I was a sinner — Islam teaches that. But no one ever explained why sin was bad. What was the consequence? What did it mean?

I moved to the U.S. and started going to church with a friend. It was nice — people were kind — but I didn't understand anything. Who is Jesus? Why do people call Him "the Light" or "the Way"? It made no sense to me.

Then someone invited me to a Bible study. Just the two of us. That second week, we read verses that changed everything. Jesus died for your past, present, and future sins.

I had heard that Jesus died for sins — but I had never understood what sin was. I stopped the study and said, "Wait. I need to understand this."

In Islam, you're told you're a sinner, but never why it matters. There's no explanation. But suddenly I understood.

Sin isn't just breaking rules. Sin wounds the heart of God. It separates us from Him — not because He's angry, but because He is holy.

I didn't have to be afraid of hell anymore. I didn't have to carry fear. Jesus had already taken my punishment.

"For Christ also suffered once for sins, the righteous for the unrighteous, that He might bring us to God" (1 Peter 3:18a).

"For by a single offering He has perfected for all time those who are being sanctified" (Hebrews 10:14).

"...while we were still sinners, Christ died for us" (Romans 5:8b).

I had peace for the first time in my life.

I called my mom and told her I loved her. Not just honored her — that I *really* loved her. I meant it. I even told her I'd die for her. That was new because I no longer feared death.

In time, my mom and sister came to believe Jesus, too. I was the first in my family to follow Jesus and now we share an eternal future.

The LORD also showed me I had to forgive my father. That was hard. I didn't want to. But one day, I got stuck in an elevator and I felt the LORD speak: "Text him. Forgive him." So I did. I told him I forgave him for everything. I said, "I love you."

That step unlocked something. We're not fully restored — but our relationship began to heal.

God changed everything — how I speak, how I dress, how I treat people. I used to never apologize. I used people. Now I try to walk in peace and humility.

What I know is this:

Jesus waited for me. For 30 years, He protected me — even when I didn't know His Name.

I read my Bible every year. Not because I understand everything, but because it's His Word. When I read it, I feel close to Him. He's still revealing Himself — and I'm still learning.

Reflection: The Kindness That Explains

Braha's story is a picture of how the LORD doesn't just call us out of sin — He explains what it is and why it separates us from Him. In a world where fear is used to control, Jesus speaks with clarity and kindness.

He didn't demand Braha's loyalty. He revealed His love — and let her choose.

"Come now, let us reason together," says the LORD. — Isaiah 1:18

"Perfect love casts out fear." — 1 John 4:18

"For Christ also suffered once for sins, the righteous for the unrighteous, to bring you to God." — 1 Peter 3:18

"By one sacrifice He has made perfect forever those who are being made holy." — Hebrews 10:14

"While we were still sinners, Christ died for us." — Romans 5:8

The Gospel is not about trying harder. It's about the One Who already did the work — and is waiting for us to receive it.

If you've ever carried fear, if you've ever wondered what sin really is, if you've ever felt too far from God to be forgiven — Braha's story is proof: Jesus waits. And when you're ready, He's still there.

Condensed Testimony (two-minutes)

I grew up in a Muslim country. My family wasn't religious, but I always carried fear — fear of dying, of hell, of never being good enough.

I came to the U.S. and started attending church with a friend. It felt good, but I didn't understand it. Then someone invited me to Bible study. That's when I read verses that changed everything. I learned that Jesus died for your past, present, and future sins.

I stopped her and said, "I don't understand sin." I had heard I was a sinner all my life — but I never knew why it mattered. That day, I understood:

Sin wounds the heart of God. But Jesus took the punishment. I didn't have to carry fear anymore.

"By one sacrifice He has made perfect forever those who are being made holy" (Hebrews 10:14).

I had peace for the first time in my life. He is making me holy.

I called my mom and told her I loved her. In time, she and my sister came to believe, too.

God also helped me forgive my father — something I never thought I'd do. Our relationship began to heal.

Now I follow Jesus. I read the Bible every year — not because I understand everything, but because it's from Him. He waited for me. And He's still revealing Himself to me in His Word.

Prayer Point

Jesus, thank You for waiting. Thank You for loving me even when I didn't know You. Forgive me for every way I've lived apart from You. Teach me what sin truly is — and what grace really means. I want to walk in Your truth, not in fear. Show me who You are.

Chapter 4

Share Like Someone Is Listening

> "Always be prepared to give an answer to everyone who asks you to give the reason for the hope that you have. But do this with gentleness and respect."
>
> — 1 Peter 3:15b NIV

So you've realized that your story matters. You believe God can use it. But what do you actually say?

That's where many believers get stuck.

Even mature Christians who've walked with the LORD for decades can find themselves caught off guard when asked, "Will you share your testimony?" We get nervous. We wonder what part to tell. We question how much detail is too much. We start trying to sound impressive or rehearsed. We get nervous and overshare, hoping the details will make it more believable - or to justify our choices. Or we clam up and say nothing at all.

Sometimes we just don't know where to begin.

Let's fix that.

Your Testimony Has a Shape

Every testimony is unique, but they all share a common structure - a before, a turning point, and an after. Think of it as three parts:

1. **Life before Christ** – What defined your life before you

encountered Him? What patterns, struggles, or mindsets were present?

2. **The moment or process of encountering Him** – What happened that revealed your need for Him? How did He make Himself known to you?

3. **Life since** – How has He changed you? What has shifted internally and externally since placing your faith in Jesus?

Whether you were saved at 7, 17, or 47, there was a before and an after. And that contrast is part of the power of your story.

Some people think they don't have a dramatic testimony. But being rescued from self-righteousness or a life of quiet control is just as much a miracle as being rescued from addiction or despair. What's more dramatic than being brought from eternal death and separation from God into eternal life? Some hesitate in sharing because they don't remember the exact moment they were saved. But the fruit of your life and the presence of transformation still tell a powerful story.

If your story sounds more like "revelation over time" than a lightning-bolt moment, that does not invalidate your testimony. Many people come to faith gradually, through a series of nudges and invitations from the Holy Spirit. The question isn't whether you remember the date. The question is whether you recognize the change - in direction, in belief, in heart.

For some, salvation comes in a single, defining moment - a clear encounter with Jesus that reorients everything. For others, it's a slower unfolding. A gradual unveiling. A quiet dawning of truth that builds over time until the heart responds with full surrender. Both are beautiful. Both are valid. Both are worth sharing.

And let's be clear: there's no such thing as a boring testimony when Jesus is at the center of it.

You are not the hero because you surrendered. Jesus is because He saved you. So your story doesn't need to be big. It needs to be true.

And the truth is always compelling.

A Clear Contrast

Your testimony doesn't just need an outline. It needs contrast.

Too often, people focus on events or behaviors rather than what was truly happening in their heart and mind. When you reflect on your life before Christ, don't just recount what happened - explore what it felt like.

Were you lonely, ashamed, striving, fearful, prideful, angry, numb, bitter, confused, self-protective, people-pleasing?

Did your life feel empty, aimless, exhausting, or out of control?

These are all markers of the "before" season. And naming them clearly helps the listener understand what has truly changed. Just as important, it helps you articulate the redemption that has taken place.

And if those emotional and spiritual realities are clear in your "before," then the "after" should reflect evidence of the opposite.

If your life before Christ was marked by shame, your after should include knowing you are fully accepted, forgiven, and loved. If you once relied on performance for worth, now you stand on the truth that you are chosen by grace. If you were bound by anxiety or control, now you walk in surrender and trust. If you once isolated yourself, now you've been placed in community and family. If you felt hopeless, you now live with eternal hope.

You are not just a better version of yourself. You are a new creation.

The before and after should mirror each other. If the before is marked by fear, the after should reflect peace. If the before was confusion, the after should reveal clarity. The contrast helps others see the transformation.

Fruit Inspection

This is not about exaggeration. It's about clarity. Your "after" should reflect the Fruit of the Spirit.

The Fruit of the Spirit is not a list to strive for - it's evidence of the life of Christ within you.

Scripture tells us plainly: "By their fruit you will recognize them" (Matthew 7:16 NIV). And Galatians 5:22–23 gives us a picture of what that fruit looks like: love, joy, peace, patience, kindness, goodness, faithfulness, gentleness, and self-control.

These aren't goals to aim for - they're evidence of a living God at work in your heart.

- **Love** shows up as security and belonging - not a need to be noticed or approved.
- **Joy** looks like deep contentment - not a temporary escape or circumstantial happiness.
- **Peace** manifests as trust in God's control - not anxiety, striving, or constant stress.
- **Patience** appears as calm under pressure - not frustration or a short spiritual fuse.
- **Kindness** flows from compassion in action - not just being nice to avoid conflict.
- **Goodness** is marked by integrity and virtue - not performance for acceptance.
- **Faithfulness** shows up in consistency and trust - not overcommitment or people-pleasing.
- **Gentleness** reveals strength under control - not passivity or weakness.

- **Self-control** reflects Spirit-led decision-making - not willpower or perfectionism.

If these traits are present - and growing - your "after" speaks powerfully of God's ongoing work in your life. Not perfectly, but consistently and with evidence.

When others see this fruit, they see what only the Holy Spirit can cultivate. And they begin to believe that transformation is possible for them, too.

How Jesus Makes Himself Known

Not everyone comes to faith in the same way.

Some people can name the exact moment - the day, time, or setting - when they recognized their need for a Savior, confessed Jesus as Lord, and surrendered their life to Him. They remember where they were sitting, what was said, even what song was playing.

Others come to faith gradually - through a series of moments and conversations, slow revelations over time. They may not remember a specific turning point, but they know that at some point, the Holy Spirit opened their eyes, softened their heart, and they responded to His call.

Both are valid. And both are testimonies of His saving grace.

If you have ever questioned the legitimacy of your salvation because you don't remember a specific date - let this be your reminder that salvation is not about remembering the moment. It's about recognizing the Savior - and surrendering to Him.

Look for the fruit. Look for the change. Look for His presence in your past - and the evidence of His Spirit in your present.

Jesus reveals Himself in different ways to different people - but always with the same purpose: to draw us into saving relationship with Him.

Know Your Audience

Just like Jesus spoke differently to the woman at the well than He did to Nicodemus, we also want to be attentive to the person or group we're speaking to. Sharing in a large gathering calls for a different tone than sitting across from someone in crisis.

When shaping your story, consider:

- Who am I speaking to?
- What do they need to know about the LORD?
- What parts of my story show His mercy, grace, or truth most clearly?
- Am I using language they'll understand?

If your listener doesn't know Christian language, avoid phrases that might confuse them. Instead of saying, "I was sanctified," you might say, "God began to change the way I thought and acted." Instead of "the LORD delivered me," say, "God gave me freedom from something I thought I'd never overcome."

The goal is not to impress - it's to invite. Your story is not a spotlight. It's a bridge.

Speak to the Listener's Deepest Need

When you know your audience, it's not just about age, background, or familiarity with Scripture — it's also about the deeper lens through which they see the world. As Jason Georges explains in *The 3D Gospel*, people often interpret life primarily through one of three cultural worldviews: guilt–innocence, shame–honor, or fear–power.

- **Guilt–Innocence:** Common in Western cultures. People are concerned with right and wrong, justice, and forgiveness. If you're speaking to someone from this worldview, they may connect most when you talk about God's forgiveness and how the blood of Jesus has cleansed you from sin.

- **Shame–Honor:** Common in many Asian, Middle Eastern, African, and Latin American contexts — and increasingly present in Western subcultures. People are deeply concerned with belonging, dignity, and restoring relationships. They may connect most when you share how God has brought you into His family, restored your worth, and covered your shame.
- **Fear–Power:** Often found in cultures with a strong awareness of spiritual forces, or in individuals who have lived in fear or under oppression. People here may resonate most when you talk about God's power to protect,

free, and give victory over what once bound you.

Your testimony may touch all three at different points, but paying attention to which lens is most important to your listener can help you emphasize the parts of your story that speak to their deepest need.

Jesus Himself did this — highlighting forgiveness to those under guilt, restoring dignity to those in shame, and demonstrating His power to those bound by fear. When you do the same, you're not changing your story; you're simply sharing it in a way that invites the listener to see Jesus as the answer to their heart's greatest need.

Discernment Requires Wisdom

Your story is powerful. But it also requires wisdom.

There are times when the Holy Spirit will lead you to share deeply and vulnerably - and times when restraint is the more loving choice. Knowing what to share, when to share it, and with whom takes maturity and prayer.

Not every detail belongs in every setting.

This is especially important when your story involves:

- **Trauma** – Sharing past trauma without context or care can trigger others or cause harm. Use discernment and avoid graphic language unless the setting truly calls for it.
- **Legal matters** – If your testimony includes past or ongoing legal issues, be cautious about what you share in public or recorded settings. Seek wise counsel if needed.
- **Mental health** – Your story may involve mental illness - yours or

someone else's. Speak with sensitivity and truth, not stigma. Avoid speaking in a way that makes you the hero. Let Jesus remain at the center.

- **Relational conflict** – Honor the dignity of others in your story, even if they hurt you. You are not required to hide the truth, but you are responsible for how you speak it. Avoid gossip, revenge-sharing, or casting blame.
- **Shock value** – It may be tempting to include dramatic or sensational details to "hook" your audience. But that's not the goal. You are not performing. You're testifying.

The Holy Spirit is your guide. He will show you when and how to share what needs to be said - and when silence or summary honors Him more.

Some Guardrails and Discernment

Discernment matters. You don't need to tell everything. You need to tell the part that is helpful, honoring to God, and appropriate for the setting.

Sharing your testimony in a prison ministry group may include different language or examples than sharing with your coworkers. Certain details - especially about abuse, trauma, or relationships - may need to be shared more sensitively depending on the audience. Oversharing can distract from the message and even cause harm if shared without care.

There are also stories that involve other people - parents, spouses, children, former partners, abusers, institutions. It's not only wise, but godly, to be mindful of how and when you include details that involve others. Prayerfully ask:

- Is this necessary to the part of the story I'm sharing?
- Am I protecting the dignity and confidentiality of others?
- Would sharing this cause unnecessary harm or trigger someone's pain?

Just because something is true doesn't mean it needs to be shared in every setting.

Again, legal circumstances, mental health diagnoses, and family trauma should be approached with Holy Spirit-led discernment. There may be moments where the LORD leads you to share those details - particularly in safe, private, or ministerial settings - but in general, it's best to focus less on the specific details of your pain and more on the specific details of God's character.

When in doubt, ask Him. The Holy Spirit is faithful to guide our tongues (Isaiah 50:4) just as He guided our hearts to salvation.

And remember: your story is still being written. You don't need to pretend you've arrived. You just need to be faithful to what God has done so far.

A Real-Life Example

Let's look at my own life.

Before I encountered Jesus, my life was marked by shame, fear, and feeling unwanted. I lived with a sense that I had to earn love or settle for what I could get. My mother practiced witchcraft. I grew up with spiritual confusion and emotional instability.

But God was already pursuing me.

My Granny was hard of hearing, so I often became her scribe - writing out things she couldn't hear clearly at church. That simple act of service became an unexpected doorway. I began absorbing the Gospel. I would listen to Christian radio programs in secret, turning the dial quietly, hungry for truth I didn't have a name for yet.

At 13, I surrendered my life to Jesus - even in the face of my mother's protest. I didn't have all the words then, but I knew this: Jesus loved me, and I wanted to follow Him.

Since then, He has placed me into family - the Body of Christ. He's brought me into community. He's shown me that I belong. He's been my healing Balm. The shame that once defined me no longer has the final word. I am not perfect. But I am His.

This wasn't just a turning point in my life— it was the moment I realized that Jesus didn't come just to improve me. He came to rescue me. I was lost in shame, self-reliance, and sin. But the Gospel made it clear: Jesus gave His life for mine, took the punishment I deserved, and rose again so that I could live free. My story began to change the day I surrendered to Him. And He's been writing every chapter since.

That's the short version. And in some settings, it's all I have time to say. But it's enough even though its not the whole story.

If I were sharing with someone from a shame-honor worldview, I would highlight how Jesus restored my dignity and gave me belonging. With someone weighed down by guilt, I would focus on His complete forgiveness. And with someone bound by fear, I would emphasize His power to free and protect me.

Questions for Reflection

1. What words or emotions describe your life before Christ?
2. How did Jesus reveal Himself to you - through a defining moment or through a gradual series of revelations?
3. What changed in your thoughts, actions, or relationships after surrendering your life to Him?

4. Which fruit of the Spirit is most evident in your life? Which do you still struggle to see?
5. What Scriptures affirm what He's done in your life?
6. What parts of your story require caution, care, or sensitivity depending on your audience?

Prayer Point

Heavenly Father, thank You for the story You are writing in my life. Jesus, help me remember what You saved me from, and rejoice in all You've done since. Teach me to tell the truth of Your goodness - not just in general, but through what You've personally done in me. Give me discernment as I share - so that others are helped, not harmed. Amen.

Chapter 5

Yarden - The Power In His Name

Yarden didn't share this story on a stage or behind a pulpit. He shared it from a place of deep honesty—quiet, unpolished, and unashamed. His journey is one of slow and steady maturing work of the Holy Spirit through dreams, deliverance, and the weight of a prophetic gift. In a world that often misunderstands the gift of prophecy, Yarden models what it looks like to stay grounded in worship, accountable in community, and surrendered to the voice of the LORD. His story reminds us that not all testimonies begin with, "I was lost"—some begin with, "I was listening."

Testimony: Yarden — Learning to Walk With, Not Just Speak For

I grew up in a house that honored the Word of God. We were a family of five—my parents, my siblings, and me—and our faith was woven into everyday life. There was worship music playing during the week, regular church attendance, and a deep reverence for Scripture. I often say I grew up knowing the Word, and that's true —but the way I experienced the LORD's presence and power didn't always match what I saw in others around me. That gap —the space between reading and hearing about God and experiencing Him— became the ground where He would shape me.

From a young age, I began to experience dreams—some encouraging, some terrifying. At first, they came with night

66

terrors or sleep paralysis. Sometimes I'd wake up drenched in sweat, disoriented, unsure if I was still dreaming. Other times, I'd wake myself up praying – saying things that felt like words that weren't my own. I didn't understand what was happening, and neither did the community around me. I had no language for it. I often felt isolated. But even amid fear, there was always one phrase that surfaced in my spirit—**Jesus loves me**. That simple refrain stayed with me, even when nothing else made sense.

In high school, I wrestled with a secret addiction to pornography, self-entitlement, and isolation that helped make feeling different "safe". It wasn't always visible on the outside. I was high performing both academically and athletically. But underneath, there was a kind of stress-fueled inner chaos. I also wrestled with same-sex attraction—not relationally, but in the way it expressed through those patterns of addiction. That only deepened my sense of being different or misunderstood, especially in my community.

One night, I had a dream that marked me. I was holding a child and running through an obstacle course set in a cave. Lava surrounded the path and I had this overwhelming sense that if I fell, or touched the wrong thing, I was going to hell. But I kept going. When I reached the end, I found my mother sitting at the cave's entrance. I prayed over her and suddenly, light filled the cave. Behind her, I saw thousands of people. That's when I realized it wasn't just about escape—it was about intercession on behalf of others.

Around that time, a worship pastor I trusted listened to my dream and gave me Andrew Murray's book *The Ministry of Intercession*. That was the first time someone helped me name what I was walking through. He told me, "I think you're called to intercede." It resonated deeply. I started to see that intercession wasn't just a moment of prayer—it was a posture of standing in the gap *with* Jesus.

The LORD also began freeing me—first from pornography, then from the deeper spiritual patterns tied to it. As that healing took root, the night terrors lessened and eventually stopped. But in telling my testimony, I began to notice something: the more I emphasized the *experience* of a dream or deliverance, the more those night terrors crept back in. The LORD revealed to me that I had started to take pride in the story, instead of pointing back to Him. That correction was hard but needed. The testimony wasn't mine to own—it was His.

Community has always mattered to me, but it hasn't always been easy. I value brotherhood and I've longed for deep spiritual connection, especially with other men. But for a while, I didn't feel fully seen. Sometimes, my dreams or expressions of the prophetic were met with confusion or discomfort. I was told to tone it down, or that it might not be real. Even though I grew up in a faith environment that embraced the Holy Spirit, there were still limitations in understanding.

Over time, I found a rhythm. I built a small circle of trusted men—a spiritual council—and stayed grounded through confession, accountability, and the Word. I began reading Scripture more intentionally, searching not just for stories, but for meaning. I started tracking themes in my dreams and comparing them to Scripture. For example, if I saw water or animals, I would ask, "Where does this appear in the Word? What might it mean?" I stopped striving for perfect interpretations and started leaning into Jesus and waiting on His understanding.

One of the most freeing truths I've learned is this: revelation is not something I can manufacture. I can ask for it, but I can't control it. I've had to yield. Sometimes the LORD speaks clearly. Sometimes He's silent. Either way, He's forming something in me.

When it comes to the prophetic, what has surprised me most is how often we treat it like a solo performance. But really, it's a shared space. The New Testament reminds us that all who believe have the Holy Spirit—so we don't hear *for* people; we hear *with* them. That changes everything. It makes the prophetic less about proving something and more about partnering with Jesus in love.

Now, I participate in a small prophetic community that meets every few months. We share what we're hearing, test it together, and stay rooted in the Word. Worship keeps me grounded. It's no longer about lyrics focused on what God has done for me—it's about Him and His Presence. I try to continually strip away anything that centers on me and keep only what points to Jesus. That's where I feel most myself and most aligned with the call on my life.

I still have dreams. Sometimes they're metaphorical. Sometimes they're intercessory. Sometimes they come in seasons of silence. But I've stopped needing to interpret everything. I've stopped yearning to be understood by everyone. And I've learned that humility is the companion of revelation.

To anyone walking with a misunderstood gift or carrying a hunger to see God move in ways that don't always fit the mold—be patient. Stay close to Jesus. Let Him do the revealing. Let Him decide the timing. He's not asking you to be impressive. He's asking you to be faithful.

And He speaks. Even in the silence.

Reflection: When the Power Isn't Yours to Carry Alone

Yarden's story carries a weight many don't talk about. Not the weight of platform or spotlight, but the private kind—when spiritual insight comes before interpretation and gifting runs ahead of understanding.

For Yarden, speaking the Name of Jesus wasn't just a line in a song—it was deliverance. In dreams that left him paralyzed or panicked, it was the *Name* of Jesus that broke the power of fear. Scripture tells us exactly why: *"God exalted Him... so that at the Name of Jesus every knee should bow..."* (Philippians 2:9–11). Whether in a pulpit or a nightmare, His Name holds all authority.

Some spiritual warfare doesn't show up on a prayer list. It shows up in the middle of the night, when your body is at rest, but your spirit is under siege. *"You will not fear the terror of night,"* Psalm 91 says— yet many of us have. And Yarden's courage reminds us that fear isn't always a failure. It can be a signal. Not to run— but to stand.

Yarden spoke candidly about growing up under a more Western, guilt/innocence framework of faith—do right, avoid wrong, confess when you fail. But what he experienced was more reflective of a *power/fear* worldview, which Scripture also names. *"The kingdom of God is not a matter of talk but of power"* (1 Corinthians 4:20 NIV), and Jesus didn't just forgive sin—*He disarmed the spiritual powers and authorities* (Colossians 2:15). Deliverance wasn't just theological—it was practical.

The tension Yarden lived with—the weight of spiritual authority, the misunderstanding of others, the loneliness of seeing things others couldn't —isn't unique to him. Many believers who sense the LORD speaking in dreams, impressions, or intercessory burdens wrestle with the same question: *Is this really from You, LORD? And if it is... why me and what do I do with it?*

There may never be an easy answer. But there is always this invitation: to stay humble, stay rooted in Scripture, and stay close to Jesus. *"God gave us a spirit not* of fear, but of power and love and self-control" (2 Timothy 1:7). And that spirit doesn't exist to make us strong for strength's sake—it exists to help us point back to Him.

If you've ever felt afraid of your own spiritual experiences—or unsure how to share them without seeming "too much"—know that you are not alone. The goal is not to perfect the gift, but to reflect the Giver. And when in doubt, look at Jesus. His words. His ways. His heart.

Because at the end of the day, *"the spirit of prophecy is the testimony of Jesus"* (Revelation 19:10). And Yarden's life reminds us that even when we feel misunderstood or unseen, Jesus never misses a moment to draw near and speak peace. Jesus shares with us so that we listen with others and stand in the gap with Jesus.

Chapter 6

Don't Leave Out the Best Part

> "Go home to your own
> people and tell them how
> much the LORD has
> done for you, and how
> He has had mercy on
> you."
>
> — Mark 5:19 NIV

If you had just five minutes to share your testimony, what would you say? What would you leave in? What would you leave out?

And would the Gospel - the actual message of salvation through Jesus - be clear?

Many believers can talk about their church background, their struggles, even their turning points. But they skip right past the Cross. They forget to say what Jesus actually did.

That's like telling someone about how you were lost in the woods and a man came to rescue you - but forgetting to mention that He carried you out on His back, treated your wounds, and gave you His own coat so you wouldn't freeze. He didn't just find you. He saved you.

And that part of the story matters most.

The Gospel Within the Testimony

When we share our testimony, we are not just giving evidence of personal change - we are pointing to the source of that change. And the source is the Gospel.

Your testimony is not the Gospel itself. But it contains the Gospel. It is a frame that reveals the greater truth:

- That all have sinned and fall short of the glory of God. (Romans 3:23)
- That the wages of sin is death, but the gift of God is eternal life in Christ Jesus our Lord. (Romans 6:23)
- That while we were still sinners, Christ died for us. (Romans 5:8)
- That if you confess with your mouth, "Jesus is Lord," and believe in your heart that God raised Him from the dead, you will be saved. (Romans 10:9)

This series of scriptures is often called the Romans Road, and it offers a simple path to understanding the message of salvation. You may not recite these verses verbatim when sharing your story - but the truths they contain should echo in your words.

Because sharing the good news of what God has done is the point.

My Testimony

Let me show you what that can look like.

I grew up in a home where there was spiritual darkness. Not just a lack of church - we were replete with occult activity. My mother practiced witchcraft. The atmosphere was heavy, confusing, and emotionally unstable. I felt unwanted. I lived under shame. I tried to earn love. I often felt like a problem or a burden.

But God was already at work.

My Granny was hard of hearing, and I became her scribe - attending church on her behalf, writing out sermon notes, and loudly sharing what happened with her. At home I'd sneak into the kitchen to pull the radio off the fridge and listen to The Urban Alternative, Focus on the Family, and Family Life Today. I was fascinated by the idea that people could actually live for

Jesus. And I was hungry for a different life.

I gave my life to Christ age 13 - even though my mother was furious. I still remember her anger, her protest. But I knew in my spirit that Jesus had saved me. I didn't have fancy language, but I had conviction. And peace after confessing I needed Jesus to save me, asking Him to come into my heart, and to be my Lord and Savior.

I wish I could say everything changed overnight. But I still struggled. I still sought approval in the wrong places. I still made sinful choices. One of those choices was staying in a relationship where I convinced myself that marriage was validated in the heart not in a piece of paper from a courthouse. I stayed for years – over 15 years - wearing rings and believing promises that never led to covenant. I kept trying to make it work. I kept trying to prove I was worthy of being loved.

But God never stopped pursuing me.

Through the conviction of the Holy Spirit and the counsel of wise believers, I surrendered that relationship. I laid it on the altar. It was one of the hardest things I've ever done. But I knew the LORD was asking me to honor Him above everyone else. And when I obeyed, He met me. He became my satisfaction. He placed me in family. He reminded me I was already chosen, already loved. He picked up the broken pieces of my shattered dreams and showed me the blessing and healing found in Him alone.

He rescued me - again.

And that's the part I almost didn't want to share. Because it wasn't tied up in a neat bow. I wasn't married at the end. I didn't get the happily-ever-after I imagined and still long for today. But I have Jesus. And He is enough.

Did you notice the arc? Shame, fear, isolation. Then rescue. Then a new identity, belonging, peace. It doesn't have to be dramatic. But it should be real.

A Note on Format

Some people worry about telling the short version of their story. Others get lost in the long version. Both are useful. Ask the Holy Spirit which to share.

Its worth mentioning again, regardless of length, your testimony will always follow the same arc:

1. Life before Christ
2. The inflection point or encounter with Him
3. Life after - marked by transformation, even if it's still in process

When you tell your story with that shape, listeners can see the Gospel reflected in your life. And it gives them hope for their own.

Just as we reflect on the story of how Jesus saved us, we can also reflect on how He continues to mature us. The same pattern of before, inflection point, and after can often be traced in stories of ongoing sanctification.

- Before – What was I believing, feeling, or doing that revealed a need for deeper surrender or healing?
- Inflection Point – What did the LORD use to confront, teach, or comfort me? What Scripture, circumstance, or moment of clarity served as the turning point?
- After – How has my heart, mindset, or behavior changed as a result of yielding to Him in that area?

This structure doesn't need to be followed rigidly, but it helps frame our testimony in a way that shows God's continued work in us. His sanctifying grace is just as powerful as His saving grace. We're not just called to be saved - we're called to be changed and transformed (Romans 12:2).

Questions for Reflection

1. What part of your testimony most clearly points to what Jesus did to save you?
2. How could you explain the Gospel inside your story so that someone else understands how they can be saved?
3. What scriptures anchor your understanding of salvation?
4. What part of your story do you tend to downplay or skip over?
5. What helps you stay focused on Jesus as the Rescuer instead of yourself?

Prayer Point

LORD, thank You for rescuing me. Thank You for dying in my place, forgiving my sin, and giving me new life. Help me never to forget the Gospel - and never to leave it out when I tell the story You gave me. Let my words always point back to You. Amen.

Chapter 7

Hosea - Slipping Yet Held

Some testimonies unfold over time. Others hit in a single moment. But often, the stories the LORD writes in our lives are too layered to tell the same way every time.

This next testimony is one of those. It's the kind of story that could be shared in a prayer circle, on a street corner, or during a quick conversation on a subway platform. And while the details stay the same, the shape of the telling may shift depending on who's listening—and how long the train takes to arrive.

So here it is: one story, shared through three windows.

Hosea — Saved Through the Fire, Kept by His Mercy

Full Testimony

Hosea grew up dutiful. He went to Catholic church because his mother asked him to – not because she was going. He studied hard because it mattered. He loved school, comics, and television. He wasn't good at making friends, but he excelled in academics, graduating near the top of his class and earning a full scholarship to a top university.

Just before he left for college, his mother became a born-again Christian. She started attending a well-known church in Manhattan and insisted that everyone in the house follow suit. Hosea went once. He didn't have much interest, but he felt something he hadn't before: a closeness to God. Later, an uncle gave him a Bible, and he took it with him to college. But once he arrived on campus, he was overwhelmed by loneliness and depression. Everyone around him seemed socially confident and emotionally mature, while he still felt like a kid inside.

At some point he fell deeply in love with a woman who moved in with him. Even in that season, conviction stirred. He began to read the Bible on his own. Without community. Without church. Without discipleship. He felt strongly that the relationship was wrong—but he didn't know what to do. He prayed daily for strength to either leave her or for her to be saved. Eventually, she cheated on him with another man. And in his words, "I was angry at God. Really angry."

In his brokenness, he moved into a dorm on campus and kept trying to seek the LORD. Hosea battled eczema so severe that it disrupted his life. One night, he called a Christian radio show for prayer.

The man on the line prayed boldly for healing and Hosea believed. But when he woke up unchanged, something snapped. That very day, he walked into the school office and withdrew from school. He was halfway through his senior year.

It was the beginning of a descent.

Back at home, Hosea was treated with contempt by his family. Isolated and desperate for connection, he began seeking friendships in his neighborhood. That search led him to drugs—not because he loved them, but because he longed for community. Pot was the price of admission. "I didn't love the drugs," he said. "I loved belonging." But addiction crept in. His mother moved away. His apartment became a space for drug use— and eventually, prostitution.

Then one day, while Hosea was out meeting a potential new employer, the police raided his apartment. He wasn't there. A woman present—herself a prostitute—defended him, saying, "God saved you today. I told them I saw a Bible in your room." Hosea later reflected, "That's the only reason nothing happened to me. God spared me."

He moved in with his brother. A friend offered him part-time work. He began stabilizing—until he got sick again. The eczema returned in force. He began fasting and praying for healing. "I gave God my most precious possession," he said—his entire Batman comic book collection. He threw it all in a dumpster and cried out for mercy.

The next day, his uncle showed up uninvited, saying he felt the LORD tell him to visit. They prayed together and went to a doctor. Hosea received treatment, and the eczema cleared within days. But once again, when healing came, he wandered. "Like the prodigal," he said, "I let the LORD clean me up, and then I went right back out."

The cycle continued. He returned to drugs, then escalated to harder ones—

cocaine, ecstasy, LSD. He experienced demonic oppression. "It was like something came in," he said, "and I wanted all the drugs, all the sex, all the darkness. It wasn't about friendship anymore. It was about the drugs."

In early adulthood, panic attacks started. One night, in a car with a drug dealer friend, he thought he was having a heart attack. The man refused to help him, afraid to get caught. That night, Hosea made a promise: "LORD, if You deliver me from drugs, I'll serve You." And God did. The desire for drugs vanished instantly.

He returned to church. He went on a mission trip to Siberia. He re-enrolled in school. But this time, the trap was alcohol. He became a functional alcoholic—serving in ministry, praying publicly, leading small groups—while drinking privately.

Eventually, in mid-life, came a turning point. "This was when I truly became a believer," he said. He confessed his alcoholism at church and attended Celebrate Recovery. He joined a fitness program in Niagara Falls—a five-week intensive sponsored by The Biggest Loser. He paid for it with his 401(k), desperate to regain health and direction. Each day, he prayed over his meals. Each week, someone approached him—strangers, fellow participants—stirred to speak with him about the LORD. In that place of physical transformation, God was working on his spirit, too. At the end of the program, a backslidden believer invited him to church, where the pastor pointed at Hosea and said, "The LORD is going to use you." And this time, Hosea believed it.

But Hosea still struggled. Not long after, he relapsed again into alcohol because of loneliness and misplaced longing. But through recovery groups, prayer, and church community, the LORD delivered him again.

Underneath it all, though, was a deeper root: sexual sin. From childhood, Hosea had been addicted to pornography. Even after being freed from drugs and alcohol, that stronghold remained. Until one day—after a moment of weakness—he was hit with a panic attack so severe he feared death.

He reached out for prayer. He confessed to mature believers. And the LORD broke it. Since that day, the craving is gone. He flees sexual temptation. He no longer plays with fire—he runs from it.

"I'm not perfect," he said. "I still struggle with food. I still battle selfishness. But I've learned to run to Jesus. And this time, I'm not letting go."

Reflection: When Deliverance Comes in Stages

Hosea's testimony is the kind that makes you stop and listen. Not because it's tidy, but because it's true. Deliverance didn't happen all at once. It came in waves. Over years. Through pain. Through panic attacks. Through relapse and repentance. And yet—Jesus never walked away.

In Psalm 107, Hosea found a mirror to his own life: "Fools, because of their transgression... draw near to the gates of death. Then they cry to the LORD in their trouble, and He delivers them..." (Psalm 107:17–20). That was his life. Again and again, he cried out. Again and again, the LORD saved him.

There's a lie that many believers wrestle with silently: If I was really saved, why do I keep struggling? But Scripture reminds us that sanctification is a process. "It is for freedom that Christ has set us free" (Galatians 5:1), but the fullness of that freedom often comes in stages. God's mercy isn't always clean or instantaneous. Sometimes it's gritty. Sometimes it shows up in the form of an uncle on your doorstep. A panic attack in a hospital bed. A word of prophecy from a stranger. Sometimes mercy is just... survival.

Hosea talked about strongholds—the kind that don't break with one prayer. He also talked about community: how isolation made everything worse, and how the Body of Christ became essential to his healing. "He who isolates himself follows his own desire..." (Proverbs 18:1). Staying in community wasn't optional. It was lifesaving.

He also told the truth about what happens when we expect miracles to look a certain way. Healing from eczema came not through the dramatic, but through the quiet kindness of medical care. And still— it was God who healed him. "Every good and perfect gift is from above..." (James 1:17).

If you've ever felt like your healing took too long—or like you've failed too many times to be used by God—take heart. The One who began a good work in you will carry it to completion (Philippians 1:6). Deliverance may not be instant. But it will be complete.

Because the mercy of God doesn't run out. It triumphed over judgment (James 2:13). And it still does.

Subway-Platform Version (90–120 Seconds)

I used to think if I messed up too many times, God would be done with me. But the truth is... He never was.

I grew up exposed to religion, but I didn't know Jesus. In college I got hit with depression and dropped out my senior year. Went home and fell into drugs—not because I loved them, but because I just wanted to belong. That turned into addiction. Then things got darker—panic attacks, demonic torment, even sexual sin.

And yet—every single time I cried out, God showed up. I'd get clean, then relapse. Go to church, then fall again. But He never gave up. Not once.

Eventually, I surrendered. The LORD set me free—first from drugs, then alcohol, and finally from the thing I thought I'd never overcome: years of hidden pornography. I run from temptation.

What I've learned is this: God's mercy doesn't expire. It chased me down. And even when I stopped believing in myself—He still did and tells me that I belong.

Elevator Version (60 Seconds)

I used to be stuck—deep in addiction, shame, panic attacks, even spiritual torment. I kept trying to fix it. But nothing worked.

I'd clean up, then fall again. Try church, relapse. But every time I cried out, Jesus met me. Not to punish me—to rescue me.

He didn't give up, even when I had. And eventually, He set me free—from drugs, alcohol, and years of hidden sin.

If you're still breathing, He's still pursuing. I'm living proof that you haven't gone too far for Jesus to reach.

Chapter 8

Not Every Story Is for Every Moment

"The Sovereign LORD has
given me a well-
instructed tongue, to
know the word that
sustains the weary."

— Isaiah 50:4a NIV

Sometimes, the most important thing you can say... is nothing at all.

Discerning when and how to share your story is just as important as knowing what to say. Every moment isn't the right moment. And every story isn't meant for every setting.

Testimonies are powerful. But they're not tools to be wielded casually. They're sacred. And when we treat them that way, we begin to notice the promptings of the Holy Spirit more clearly.

When the LORD Says, "Tell Them What I Did"

There have been times when I clearly felt prompted to share part of my testimony. Usually it happened when I could see someone struggling in an area I knew personally - family dysfunction, spiritual confusion, cohabitation outside of marriage, shame. I didn't always jump in right away. Sometimes I hesitated. Not because I was ashamed, but because I didn't want to center myself or get in the way of what the Holy Spirit was already doing.

But in those moments, the LORD would nudge me: Tell her what I did.

I remember a young woman I was discipling. She was in crisis, and I could relate. Because of a conflict with her parents, she'd moved in with her boyfriend - both of them active in the church. I had lived with a man for many years, waiting on promises of marriage that never came. I convinced myself that marriage was just a piece of paper. That Adam and Eve didn't have a license. But I knew deep down that I wasn't walking in God's best. I was coping, not trusting.

Eventually, I laid that relationship down. It took more than a decade. The decision to walk away wasn't about reclaiming my dignity. It was about surrendering my desires and dreams to the One Who died for me. The Gospel isn't just for salvation —it's for sanctification. Jesus didn't just save me once—He keeps saving me, shaping me, and drawing me closer to Himself. Even when the consequences of my choices linger, His grace is deeper still. This is the power of the Gospel at work in real life.

When I shared that with her - not as judgment, but as testimony - she heard the LORD for herself. She moved out the same day. They married the following week. And they're still married now, more than a decade later and serving in ministry.

It wasn't my story that redeemed her situation. It was Jesus and His redeeming grace. But He used my obedience to speak to her heart from my own life of redemption in the specific area of offering ourselves as living sacrifices to the Lord (Romans 12:1).

> "Faith comes by hearing,
>   and hearing through the
>   word of Christ."
>
> — Romans 10:17

From Fear to Reverence

When I first began sharing my testimony aloud, I noticed that I was unusually nervous. It was strange because I speak in public as a core part of my career. I later recognized it as anxiousness. At first, I was afraid. I was afraid that people would define me by my past, despite knowing that Jesus had forgiven me. I was afraid of being rejected.

Over time, that fear turned into reverence. As I practiced sharing my testimony with Jesus at the center - as the Rescuer, not me - I stopped focusing on shame. I stopped worrying about performance. And I started standing in awe that He would not only save and purify someone like me - but also invite me to tell others about it.

> "Sharing our struggles and our failures can be just as powerful as sharing our victories and successes, because it shows others that sanctification is an ongoing process that requires ongoing surrender and growth."
>
> — Tim Keller, 2016, p. 198

That is still stunning to me. Every time.

What About the Story That's Still Unfolding?

One of the biggest lies the enemy tells us is this: You can't share until it's tidy, healed, or happy. But God was glorified even as Paul shared from prison. It was still messy—but Jesus was magnified in the middle of it.

The truth is, the LORD often uses our in-process stories to reach people who feel stuck in their own not-yet-finished story. You don't have to pretend to be further along than you are. But you do need to be honest about what God has done so far - and what you're trusting Him for next.

We live in the tension of "already but not yet." He has saved us. And He is still sanctifying us. We are forgiven. And we are still being transformed from one degree of glory to the next (2 Corinthians 3:18).

Sharing from that place of humility and honesty doesn't disqualify your story. It magnifies His grace and mercy.

Questions for Reflection

1. Have you ever felt the Holy Spirit prompting you to share part of your story? What happened?
2. What helps you discern whether a moment is right to share or not?
3. Have you ever regretted sharing too much - or too little? What did you learn?
4. What story of His faithfulness are you still waiting to tell? What's your not-yet-finished story of hope?
5. How has your reverence for sharing your testimony changed over time?

Prayer Point

Holy Spirit, thank You for trusting me with the story Jesus is writing in my life. Teach me when to speak and when to stay silent. Give me discernment, compassion, and courage. Help me be a faithful witness - whether I'm planting seeds, watering, or watching You bring the growth. Amen.

Chapter 9

Dillon – The Long Road Home

I grew up in church. I knew the Gospel early, sat under good Bible teaching, even preached on Youth Sundays as a teenager. When I was nine years old, I walked the aisle during an altar call and was baptized two weeks later. But the truth is, there was no real life change. I knew the right words. I knew how to sound like a believer. I could flip the switch and wear the part like a coat. But underneath, nothing had been surrendered.

My home life was complicated. My father was an alcoholic—sometimes sober, often not—and my mother battled depression. As the oldest child, I felt a responsibility to hold things together. At church, we looked like any other family. At home, things were falling apart. There was tension, instability, and a quiet ache for something more. That upbringing trained me to perform—especially when it came to faith. If you'd looked at me then, you might've seen someone devout. But the real work of God hadn't yet begun in me.

When I went to college, I felt a kind of release—like I could finally step away from the chaos of home. I distanced myself from family, but also from God. Even then, I didn't think of myself as far from Him. I was just doing life. But in hindsight, I was drifting.

It wasn't until my late 20s—married, with two young daughters—that everything started to change. We lived around the corner from a small church, and a neighbor invited us to bring the kids to VBS. I didn't want to go. I was always traveling, always busy. I didn't feel like I had the time to be away from my family. But my wife, said, "We're taking them." So we did.

I'll never forget sitting on the second row on the right-hand side of that little church during the closing program. It felt like I was the only person in the room. The presence of God met me there. I wept. That was the beginning—the moment He truly got my attention. That was when I fully trusted in Christ.

From that point forward, my faith wasn't just something I could explain. It became something I lived. The change was gradual, but it was real. My desires shifted. My priorities reoriented. And in time, I realized that even though I had been baptized at nine, I needed to be baptized again—as an act of obedience, now that I understood surrender. That obedience wasn't about performance. It was about trusting God's order: believe, surrender, and then respond.

Even now I still, I struggle. I'm a doer, a fixer, an organizer. I like to take action, to solve problems, to keep things moving. But the Lord kept pressing something deeper: Will you trust Me when I ask you not to act? Will you pray instead of fix? Wait instead of work? It's one of the hardest things for me —this daily wrestling with sovereignty. What does He want me to do versus what does He want me to entrust to Him alone?

Even now, decades later, I feel that tension. I teach in a Christian school. I serve as an elder. I read Scripture, pray, and walk with the LORD. But the old instincts creep in. I catch myself "checking boxes"—not out of love, but out of rhythm or habit. I'll find myself flipping the switch again when I'm in public, putting on a voice or posture that may not match what's happening in my heart.

But God is patient. His sovereignty doesn't just govern the world—it governs my sanctification. He draws me back.

Again and again, when my mind wanders or my discipline fades, He says, Come back. I'm not done with you yet.

Lately, the book of Titus has been confronting me. I've read it many times before, but recently I felt the LORD tell me to return to it. And not just skim— to soak. Over and over again, I kept rereading the qualifications for an elder. Am I above reproach? Am I sober-minded? Am I self-controlled? I don't want to breeze past those words—I want them to shape me.

Sovereignty has become the thread that ties everything together for me. I believe with all my heart that God is working in all things. Even when I don't understand His timing or methods, I trust His hand. I know now that He didn't save me because I was good, or because I had potential, or because I earned it. He saved me because He is good. It was His initiative. His mercy. His glory.

To anyone who sees the world through the lens of checklists and expectations, who wonders if they've missed the mark—remember this: your good works won't save you. But they do glorify the One who did. I needed to get the order right—salvation first, then obedience, then the daily surrender of being shaped by His Spirit.

And sometimes, the most obedient thing I can do... is pray.

Reflection: Getting the Order Right

For some of us, the battle isn't against rebellion—it's against performance. Not open defiance, but quiet striving. Dillon's story reminds us that you can grow up in church, serve in ministry, speak the Gospel fluently... and still miss the point of being yielded to Him. Not because you're faking it, but because surrender hasn't taken root.

He spoke of knowing the right words as a teenager—how to turn on the "church voice," how to flip the switch when needed. But it wasn't until his 20s, when he sat in a little church watching a VBS program for his kids, that the LORD truly got his attention. The room fell away. The tears came. And with them came a new kind of knowing—not just about Jesus, but a surrender to Him.

One word kept surfacing as Dillon spoke: sovereignty. Not as a theological concept alone, but as the lived tension of asking, Do I act, or do I wait? Do I organize, or do I pray? That tension is real for anyone who's wired as a doer—someone who equates faithfulness with productivity. But the Bible is clear: "The LORD will fight for you; you need only to be still" (Exodus 14:14). And at other times: "Go, for I am sending you" (Judges 6:14). Obedience, not outcome, is what matters.

Dillon's story also addresses something many believers struggle with quietly: the fear of what people will think. What if they see me get baptized again? What if they think I got it wrong the first time? But Scripture says: "Man looks at the outward appearance, but the LORD looks at the heart" (1 Samuel 16:7). It's not legalism to follow God's order. Legalism says do this to earn love. Obedience says do this because you're already loved.

He was honest about falling into patterns —checking boxes, drifting into routine, flipping on the teacher/elder mode out of habit. But he was equally honest about how the LORD draws him back. Sovereignty doesn't mean passivity. It means trusting that the God who saves is also the God who sanctifies and transforms. "It is God who works in you to will and to act according to His good purpose" (Philippians 2:13).

We are not saved by what we do. But we are saved to do good works—works that don't point to us, but to the One who gave Himself for us (Ephesians 2:8-10). That's what Dillon discovered in Titus, and it's what Scripture affirms over and over again: the Spirit of God produces the life of God in the people of God.

If you've ever wrestled with whether your life "measures up," hear this: You're not the measure. Jesus is. And He is faithful. Even when we wander, He draws us back. Again and again. Because this isn't about keeping score—it's about being shaped by grace.

Chapter 10

Jesus Prayed for Their Faith - And Your Words

> "My prayer is not for them
> alone. I pray also for
> those who will believe in
> Me through their
> message."
>
> — John 17:20 NIV

There is something deeply humbling about these words. Jesus, the Son of God, prayed for the people who would believe in Him - not just through His miracles, not just through His death and resurrection, but through the testimonies and stories of those who followed Him.

He prayed for your message.

He prayed for your words.

He prayed for the person who will one day believe in Him because you shared what He did in *your* life.

Preparation Is an Act of Faith

Preparing to share your testimony is not performance - it's an act of faith. It says, "I believe there will be a moment, ordained by God, where someone will need to hear the story He gave me. And I want to be ready."

It's not about memorizing a script. It's about cooperating with the Holy Spirit to recall what God has done and communicate it with clarity.

Jesus doesn't need your perfection. But He does invite your participation.

What Keeps Us From Preparing?

Sometimes we don't prepare because:

- We don't feel "ready" yet
- We're afraid our story is unfinished
- We're waiting for a "better" version of our life
- We think it's someone else's job

Other times, we feel unqualified or uncertain. But remember you don't need a microphone or a ministry title. You just need willingness.

When we prepare, we're saying, "Here I am, LORD. Use me."

Why Language Matters

When I refer to "my story," I'm really talking about God's story in my life. That's intentional. It may sound longer or less catchy, but it reflects something deeply theological:

- I'm not the author of my testimony - He is
- I'm not the hero of the story - Jesus is
- I'm not amplifying my truth - I'm pointing to His truth

It's countercultural. But so is the Gospel.

Some alternatives you'll find in this book include:

- "the story He gave me"
- "the story God is writing in your life"
- "His story of redemption in your life"

This shift isn't about semantics. It's about stewardship.

And it reorients the purpose of your testimony. You're not spotlighting yourself.

You're testifying to the Author and Finisher of your faith (Hebrews 12:2).

Questions for Reflection

1. What is the last thing God clearly did in your life that you want to remember or share?
2. What's one example of Jesus meeting you in your weakness?
3. Where do you still feel "unfinished," and how does that make you hesitate to share?
4. How has your testimony grown deeper over time?
5. Have you ever regretted sharing too much or too little? What did you learn from that?
6. What Scriptures affirm the story God is writing in your life?

Prayer Point

LORD, thank You that You prayed for those who would believe through the message You entrusted to us. Help me prepare - not out of pressure, but out of faith. Teach me how to tell the story You've written in my life with clarity and reverence, so that others may see You and believe. Amen.

Chapter 11

Gwen – Found in the Ruins

Some stories carry more than pain — they carry patterns. Generational trauma. Cycles of violence and abuse that feel impossible to escape. Gwen's story is one of those. But it's also a story of interruption. Of the LORD stepping in — again and again — even when she didn't know how to ask. She doesn't tell her story to be pitied. She tells it because she knows Who brought her through it. And that same God is still healing, still rescuing, and still writing redemptive stories today.

Let's look at a long and short version of this complex story. ***This story contains mention of familial violence and trauma. Discretion is advised for sensitive readers.***

Gwen's Testimony

Gwen was nine years old when her father murdered her mother. He turned himself in. She was sent into foster care — but instead of safety, she encountered more trauma. From the age of 9 to 17, she was sexually abused in multiple foster homes. "I was an atheist," she said. "I didn't let anyone talk to me about God. I would stop them right there — 'If God is real, why would He let this happen to me?'"

At 17, she spent 2.5 years in a jail for violence. After her release, she became involved in the drug trade, entangled with cartels. She lived dangerously and didn't care about consequences. "I was addicted to danger. I had no fear," she said.

When she became pregnant at 19 — despite being told she couldn't have children — it caught her off guard. "It was a miracle," she said. "I didn't want kids. I never planned for them. But something about that pregnancy slowed me down." Her son's father wasn't a believer, but his family was. They introduced her to faith gently. Out of curiosity, she began reading the Bible after buying a large coffee-table Bible from a door-to-door salesman.

Still, church was complicated. A visit to one congregation ended with a pastor making advances. "That did it for me," she said. "I told God He could be in my heart, but I was never stepping into another church." But God had other plans. For years, she carried a Bible in her purse — not because she understood it, but because it felt like a shield.

Meanwhile, she battled addiction to prescription opiates — a dependency that began after a bone marrow biopsy in her twenties. "I was on heavy meds for a while. I was chewing them just to make the pain stop faster."

One day, after a dental visit, she overdosed — unintentionally taking 16 pills. She looked in the mirror and saw her skin turning blue. "I didn't want to go to the hospital. I was scared they'd take my son," she said. Then she heard, clearly, what she describes as divine instruction: "Go drink milk. Go vomit." She obeyed. Then she heard: "Count the pills." That's when she realized how much she had taken. She was in danger.

She detoxed at home — alone, for three weeks. The withdrawal was brutal. "My bones felt like they were breaking," she said. "I couldn't stand, couldn't shower, couldn't eat. Just me and my son in the house. He helped cook. The LORD was closing every door."

She finally went to the hospital because she began to bleed and thought she was going to die. There, alone in a hospital room, she prayed: "LORD, I don't want my son to go through what I did. If You save me, I'll serve You." She didn't know where the words came from. But from that moment, everything began to shift. God heard and answered.

Gwen found Jesus. She found a church. She shared her love for cooking by cooking for others. She began feeding the homeless. "I didn't know how to evangelize," she said. "The LORD taught me." She bought 40-pound bags of chicken, cooked meals, and delivered food — along with Scripture and prayer — to those on the streets. She began to see what others couldn't. "I asked the LORD to let me see how He sees, feel what He feels."

Gwen's story is still unfolding. But if there's one thing she knows: "God is love," she said. "Nobody ever gave me love — not real love. He was the first One. He gave me His eyes, His heart. I used to say, 'I don't want to feel (or live) anymore,' but now I feel what other people are going through."

Reflection: The Cycle Ends with Jesus

Gwen's story could have been a statistic. Trauma after trauma. Addiction. Violence. Even two suicide attempts. Her own father took her mother's life — just like his father had done before him. That kind of generational sin doesn't break easily.

But God doesn't need easy. He just needs access.

Jesus met Gwen when she didn't want to be met. When she was hostile to faith. When she carried a Bible like an amulet, not a promise. When she was convinced the church had nothing for her. And yet — in hospital rooms and prison, through a door-to-door Bible sale and an unplanned pregnancy — He kept showing up.

"The LORD is near to the brokenhearted and saves the crushed in spirit" (Psalm

34:18). He's not afraid of your mess. He's not waiting for a cleaned-up version of your life. Gwen's story proves that.

And maybe, like her, you've asked: "Where were You when it hurt?" She asked that too. The LORD didn't excuse the evil done to her — He named it for what it was. Yet even there, He was not absent. He walked her back through those memories — slowly, gently — showing her that His sovereignty had preserved her life, His truth had spoken against the darkness, and His presence had carried her when she could not carry herself. He wept with her pain, even as He promised that injustice will not have the last word.

This is the Gospel:

- For the shamed, Jesus restores dignity.
- For the fearful, Jesus carries power and peace.
- For the guilty, Jesus offers mercy and freedom.

"It is for freedom that Christ has set us free" (Galatians 5:1). And that freedom can begin today — even while your story is still being written.

Condensed Version (two-minutes, first person)

I was nine when my father murdered my mother. From there, it was foster homes and abuse. I shut down emotionally. I didn't let anyone talk to me about God. If He was real, why would He let all that happen?

I got violent. I went to prison. I got into drugs, into organized crime. But then I got pregnant — even though I'd been told I could never have kids. I now know that unplanned child was part of what the LORD used to slow me down.

After a medical procedure, I became addicted to prescriptions pain killers. One day I overdosed. Took 16 pills. I looked in the mirror and saw myself turning blue. I heard, "Go drink milk. Go vomit." And somehow, I survived. I detoxed at home for three weeks. Couldn't stand. Couldn't shower. Couldn't eat. Just my son and me — and God. After three weeks, I started to bleed and went to the hospital, I prayed: "LORD, if You save me, I'll serve You." I didn't even know what I meant. But He took me at my word. Jesus rescued me.

Since then, He's taught me how to love. I started feeding the homeless, praying in hospitals, evangelizing on the streets. Not because I had training. Just because I asked: "LORD, help me see as You see."

I used to say, "I don't want to feel anymore." Now, I feel what others carry — and I know the LORD's heart for them. Because I've lived it.

He is love. And He never stopped pursuing me.

Chapter 12

The LORD Has Done Great Things for Us

> Then our mouth was filled with laughter, and our tongue with shouts of joy; then they said among the nations, "The LORD has done great things for them." The LORD has done great things for us; we are glad.
>
> — Psalm 126:2-3

Why do we share our testimony? Because the LORD has done great things for us.

It's that simple.

It's also that sacred.

The story of what God has done in your life is not just a reflection of the past - it's a signpost for others. A pointer. A declaration that He is still saving, healing, restoring, forgiving, and transforming lives today.

And someone is waiting to hear it.

Faith Is Personal - But Never Private

There's a popular idea that faith is "a private matter." And while it's true that our relationship with Jesus is deeply personal - it was never meant to be kept hidden.

Your testimony is not just for you. It's for others. It's for the people Jesus prayed for in John 17 - the ones who would come to believe because of the message you share.

We often think about the Great Commission in terms of preaching or evangelizing. But sharing your testimony is one of the most accessible ways to make Jesus known.

It doesn't require a platform. Just a moment. A conversation. A willingness.

And when you speak, something powerful happens.

> "Let the redeemed of the
> LORD tell their story -
> those He redeemed from
> the hand of the foe."
>
> — Psalm 107:2 NIV

Testimony in Everyday Life

Sharing your story doesn't always look like standing in front of a crowd. It might look like:

- A conversation with a coworker who's struggling
- A quiet moment with a friend in crisis
- A text message or voice memo to encourage someone
- A short post on social media
- A reply to someone who says, "You seem different - what changed?"

You don't need to force it. Just be ready. And when the Holy Spirit nudges you, respond with humility and clarity

Sometimes you'll share the full arc. Other times, just a thread. Either way, your words matter.

Because they testify of the LORD's redeeming power and love.

Prepare and Respond with Faithfulness

Before you share your testimony, prepare your heart.

Ask the Holy Spirit to lead. Surrender any fear of rejection or desire to impress. This is not about how well you speak - it's about Who you speak of.

You may want to write down your story. Practice aloud. Ask a trusted friend or someone living out the kind of faith you want to grow into. Share and allow them to listen and give feedback. But more than anything, ask the LORD to prepare the heart of the hearer - because He already knows who will be listening.

> My prayer is not for them alone. I pray also for those who will believe in Me through their message.
>
> — John 17:20

After you share, don't obsess over how it was received.

Some people may be deeply moved. Others may ask hard questions. Some might say nothing at all. You are not responsible for the outcome. You are responsible for the obedience.

And if someone disagrees - or tries to challenge your story - remember: your testimony is not an argument. It is not apologetics. It is not a theological debate.

You are not sharing to win. You are sharing to witness.

Jesus doesn't need you to defend Him. He invites you to represent Him.

Speak plainly. Answer gently. And when in doubt - let the Holy Spirit carry what you said deeper than words ever could.

Sharing online brings its own set of challenges. If you post a testimony or story digitally - keep it brief, clear, and Christ-centered. Avoid vague "inspirational" language. Speak plainly of Jesus, not just "faith" or "good vibes." And if comments come - whether supportive, confused, or critical - respond with grace or not at all.

You are planting seeds. The Holy Spirit waters them. Let Him be the One Who brings the fruit.

Be Ready for Responses

Not everyone will receive your story with joy. Some will be curious. Others skeptical. A few may push back.

That's okay.

You are not responsible for how people respond. You are responsible for being faithful to share what He's done.

When someone disagrees, don't argue. When they ask questions, answer with grace. When they're moved, listen well. And when they say nothing at all, trust that seeds have still been planted.

As Jen Wilkin says:

> "The heart cannot love what
> the mind does not know."
>
> — Wilkin, 2016, p. 81

Your testimony helps others know what He's like. And knowing Him leads to loving Him.

Questions for Reflection

1. As you read this book, did someone come to mind who might need to hear what God has done in your life?
2. What spaces has God placed you in where your story might open a door?
3. How do you tend to respond when people ask about your faith?
4. What hesitations still remain?
5. What would it look like to surrender hesitation to the LORD?

Prayer Point

LORD, You have done great things for me. And I want to share them. Not to glorify myself, but to make You known. Give me boldness where I am hesitant, and gentleness where I am tempted to be defensive. Let my testimony be a light that points others to You. Use it for Your glory. Amen.

Chapter 13

Mireya — When Your Process Looks Different

Some testimonies are still in process and unfolding — but that doesn't mean God is absent. Even in stories that are still unfolding, the character of God can already be seen — steady, faithful, and near. This is one of them.

Mireya didn't grow up with faith. She didn't have a church background, a salvation date, or a clear before-and-after story. But she does have moments — specific, unforgettable points in time — where she believes the LORD was speaking. Revealing. Pursuing. She doesn't claim to have every answer, but she's still listening. And through her honesty, the heart of Jesus comes into view.

God's Story in Mireya's Life

Mireya wasn't raised in the church. There was no regular mention of God in her home. Her family didn't practice any kind of faith. The only spiritual reference she recalls was seasonal — the kind of reverence reserved for playing Handel's Messiah at Christmastime.

As a child, she once learned in Catholic school to pray silently when an ambulance passed. It became a habit — a way to acknowledge suffering she couldn't see. But when she did it in the car with her parents, she was scolded. It was a moment she never forgot. Another time, someone gave her a rosary. She was told to return it. "That wasn't something we welcomed in our house," she said.

Later, she was sent to visit extended family who were more religious — but the experience left her questioning and curious. "They had lots of rules and restrictions and believed prophets who weren't in the Bible," she recalled. "They would speak things over me, or call people prophets, and I didn't know what any of it meant." It didn't draw her closer to God. It made her uncertain. The language of faith felt unfamiliar — and distorted. Especially because of all the mention of denominations – none of which is in the Bible.

As she got older, Mireya became aware of patterns — impressions, phrases, and moments that seemed connected. "I started noticing signs," she said. "Things would happen that felt like they were trying to get my attention." She didn't know who to talk to about it. She started writing things down to make sense of it all, to research, and to remember.

At one point, the intensity of what she was experiencing overwhelmed her. She described being in a state where she couldn't tell what was from God and what wasn't. Eventually, she was hospitalized. "It was a very confusing time," she said. "I knew something real was happening, but I didn't know how to explain it."

Since then, she's continued to observe, to reflect, and to write. She describes multiple moments — inflection points — where she believes God revealed Himself to her. Each time, the circumstances were deeply personal, often during periods of crisis. But what struck her most was the improbability of it all. She's a data-driven thinker, someone who values logic and research. And the things she saw and heard — the way events aligned — felt too statistically impossible to dismiss.

She's drawn to Jesus — particularly the way He loves the overlooked and the outcast. "That part of Him resonates with me," she said. "It feels familiar." She doesn't claim a label or a specific salvation moment, but she's seeking. She's still testing. Still paying attention to the patterns she sees and the truth she longs to find. And beneath it all, she carries a deep reverence and fear of God — a quiet caution that keeps her honest in the search what is true and right.

Reflection: God Is Not Threatened by Your Questions

We often expect testimonies to follow a certain pattern: lost, found, transformed. But what about the stories that don't fit that mold? What about those still seeking — still testing, still asking? Does God wait on the other side of belief, or does He meet us in the mystery as faith is growing and unfolding?

Mireya's story reminds us that the LORD is not offended by process. In fact, Scripture tells us plainly: "You will seek

Me and find Me when you seek Me with all your heart" (Jeremiah 29:13). That promise doesn't come with fine print. It doesn't require polished theology or a dramatic moment — but it does require a response. Seeking is part of the journey. Surrender to Jesus is what changes everything.

There's something sacred about Mireya's integrity. She doesn't want to perform belief. She wants to know what's real. She's not content with surface answers. She pays attention. She tests what she hears. "Test everything; hold fast to what is good" (1 Thessalonians 5:21).

And still — the LORD has been drawing near. Not once. Not vaguely. But repeatedly — in specific, undeniable moments. In the places where her world felt unstable, God showed up. And not just emotionally — but with tangible, verifiable confirmation that challenged her analytical mind. God speaks in a language we can hear. And for Mireya, that has included both mystery and measurable validation.

She's especially drawn to how Jesus loves the marginalized. That part of His character makes sense to her — because it's how He's met her, too. Gently. Consistently. Without shame. With compassion.

And maybe, as you've read her story, you recognize something of your own. Maybe you've also felt the pull of something true — but haven't known what to do with it.

Here's what the Gospel offers, no matter your background:

- If you've ever felt ashamed, unseen, or out of place, Jesus came to restore your honor and call you family. (Romans 10:11 – "Whoever believes in Him will not be put to shame")
- If you've ever felt afraid, spiritually oppressed, or powerless, Jesus

came to rescue and protect you under His Name. (Luke 10:17–20 – "Even the demons submit to us in Your Name")

- If you've ever felt guilty or burdened by regret, Jesus took your place so you could stand forgiven and free. (2 Corinthians 5:21 – "He made Him who knew no sin to be sin for us")

You don't have to clean yourself up first. You don't have to get everything right.

But you do have to respond.

Prayer for Those Still Seeking

LORD, I don't have all the answers.

I don't know how to sort out every voice I've heard or every feeling I've felt.

But I want to know what's real.

I want to know You.

If You've been speaking — help me recognize it.

If You've been pursuing — help me stop running.

Jesus, You Are Who You say You are - help my unbelief so I can trust You.

Not because I'm pressured, but because it's true.

Forgive me for the ways I've resisted and demanded to know more.

Set me free from anything false - protect me from being deceived.

Cover my shame. Break the grip of fear that I'd believe a lie.

And give me the courage to take the next step — even if I still have questions.

I may not have every answer, but I believe You are worth trusting.

I need You.

And because You are who You say You are
—

I say yes to You, Jesus.

Amen.

Chapter 14
A Final Word

You don't have to be a preacher.

You don't have to have the gift of evangelism.

You don't even have to feel fully ready.

You just have to be willing.

The LORD has entrusted you with a story - not to hide it, but to steward it. A story that's not ultimately about you, but about Jesus - the One Who saved, healed, rescued, and is still at work in your life.

Someone is waiting to hear what Jesus has done.

You were never called to save the world - but you are called to point to the One Who did. After all, salvation belongs to Him (Psalm 3:8).

And when you do, the Holy Spirit will do the rest.

Go boldly.

Go gently.

Go in His Name.

You are not alone.

Facilitator's Guide

If you're reading this section, it means you've said yes to something significant.

You've stepped into the role of helping others reflect on, articulate, and share the story God is writing in their lives. You're not expected to be a pastor, counselor, or expert. You're a guide. A companion. A fellow traveler. And you've been entrusted with the holy ground of helping others bear witness to the work of Jesus in their lives.

That's no small thing.

The Role of a Facilitator

Your goal isn't to teach every detail or have all the answers. Your role is to:

- Create a safe, Spirit-led space where people can explore what the LORD has done in their lives
- Model humility and reverence as you share your own journey
- Gently guide conversation by asking questions that promote discovery
- Encourage preparation without performance
- And always, always point people back to Jesus - the Author and Finisher of every testimony

Flexible Format

This material can be used in a variety of ways:

- A multi-week small group or discipleship study
- A weekend retreat or intensive workshop
- A testimony prep course for baptism, discipleship, or evangelism training
- A personal study guide

Adapt it to the needs of your group. There's no one-size-fits-all formula.

Creating Safety

- Open with prayer, and invite the Holy Spirit to lead
- Honor the pace of the group - some may be ready to share quickly, others will need time
- Never force vulnerability
- Remind participants that their story is still being written - and that it's okay if some parts feel unresolved

- If someone shares something especially painful or complex, gently encourage them to speak with a trusted church leader or pastoral care team

A Word on Discernment

Facilitating this content means holding space for real, sometimes messy, parts of people's lives. That's holy work - and it's also weighty. Remember, your job is not to "fix" or advise. It's to reflect Christ's compassion, listen well, and steward the time wisely.

The questions provided in this guide are designed to prompt reflection, connection, and spiritual growth. Use them as a framework, not a checklist.

And Above All

Remember: Jesus is the center of every testimony. Every story worth telling is ultimately about Him.

When someone shares about freedom from addiction, restored relationships, protection from harm, or quiet transformation over time - point it back to the goodness of God. Celebrate His work, not our performance.

We don't share to be seen. We share because we've been saved. And because someone out there needs to hear what the LORD has done.

Acknowledgments

To the Author of every good story — thank You, Abba. Father, You have been patient, gentle, kind, ever-present, and trustworthy. Thank You for writing what I could never write on my own and for using me as a pen.

Jesus, You are the center of every true story. Thank You for redeeming what was broken, for standing in the gap, and for showing us how to love and steward what You've given without fear.

Holy Spirit, thank You for breathing life into these pages — for leading, prompting, convicting, and comforting all along the way.

To Pastor Justin Lewandowski — thank you for lending your voice and your heart to the foreword of this book. Your shepherd's care, your example of humble leadership, and your faithful presence have shaped more than just these pages.

To the ones who prayed in silence, encouraged in passing, and stood behind the scenes — your intercession and quiet support carried me farther than you know. And to the one who reminded me to honor the pace of the Lord, not just the pressure to finish — thank you. Your voices helped me stay faithful to the process, not just the finished pages.

To those who shared your stories so vulnerably — thank you. You trusted me to listen, to carry your voice with care, and to point the glory back to God. Your honesty, faith, and process are a gift.

To every unseen hand, whispered prayer, and quiet word of encouragement — this book bears your fingerprints, too.

All glory to the Father, Son, and Holy Spirit — forever faithful, always worthy.

Bibliography

Cymbala, J. (1997). Fresh wind, fresh fire: What happens when God's spirit invades the heart of his people. Zondervan.

Georges, J. (2014). *The 3D Gospel: Ministry in guilt, shame, and fear cultures*. Timē Press.

Keller, T. J. (2016). Making sense of God: An invitation to the skeptical. Viking.

Murray, A. (1898/1981). *The ministry of intercession: A plea for more prayer*. Bethany House Publishers.

Wilkin, J. (2016). None like Him: 10 ways God is different from us (and why that's a good thing). Crossway.

About the Author

La'Treall *(luh-TRELL)* Maddox is an executive leader and founder of Ox & Maven, where she serves as a strategic partner to mission minded leaders helping them turn complexity into clarity and measurable

Photo by J.J. Fecik @jjfecik

action. Her career spans finance, strategy, risk, and executive leadership, with thought leadership publications through Oxford University and ITSMF Press. Her chapter, The Power of Not Knowing, appears in *A Dream Realized: Essays on Leadership, Triumphs, and Truths*.

Stewarding God's Story in Your Life reflects the same foundation that has guided her leadership in the corporate world — the conviction that every story God writes shapes how we show up, make decisions, and serve others. This first long-form personal project is centered on the power of testimony and the way God redeems and writes every chapter of our lives.

She is a speaker, teacher, and writer committed to biblical literacy. Her love for God's Word shapes her work, her writing, and her relationships. Whether helping leaders clarify vision in the boardroom or opening God's Word in the living room, she believes every believer is called to steward the story God is writing in their life.

She lives in New York City, where her mornings begin in stillness — just her, a warm drink in hand, her retired guide dog, Lily, at her feet, and time in the Word. She delights in the gift of family, both by birth and by choice, finding in them her greatest earthly joys and glimpses of God's redemption in what she once longed for was a child. Though she treasures solitude, she loves welcoming others into her home — a place often filled with laughter, shared meals, and the kind of fellowship that nourishes both body and soul. She delights in doing life with others across generations — from unhurried conversations after church to lingering hours in coffee shops, often in search of the perfect paleo spicy chai — and lingering until servers are wiping down counters for closing.

To learn more or get in touch, visit www.oxandmaven.com.

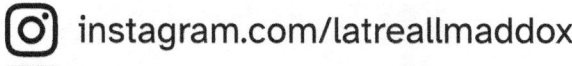 instagram.com/latreallmaddox
linkedin.com/in/lmaddox